FIRST STEPS IN ART APPRECIATION

The last date stamp is the date of issue.

- 8. MAR. 1962	24. JUL. 1971		
28. MAR. 1962			
26. APR. 1962			
- 6. SEP. 1962			
22. DEC. 1962			
14. JUN. 1963			
17. SEP. 1963			
28. OCT. 1963			
18. JAN. 1964			
20. OCT. 1964			
24. OCT. 1964 22. DEC. 1964			
18. JAN. 1965			
- 6. MAR. 1965			
- 5. AUG. 1965			
19. AUG. 1965			
29. SEP. 1965			
25th Oct 66			
- 8. JUN. 1968			
13. JUL. 1968			
31. DEC. 1969			
- 7. DEC. 1970			

La Montagne Sainte Victoire by Cézanne.   *Courtauld Institute*
(See page 26)

FIRST STEPS
IN ART
APPRECIATION

Nika Hulton

PHOENIX HOUSE LTD

LONDON

© NIKA HULTON, 1958

Printed in Great Britain
in 14 point Monotype Bembo by
The Chiswick Press, New Southgate N.11 for
Phoenix House Ltd, 38 William IV Street,
Charing Cross, W.C.2

First Published 1958

CONTENTS

LIST OF ILLUSTRATIONS

IN COLOUR

IN MONOCHROME (*between pages* 32 *and* 33)

FOREWORD

THIS SHORT BOOK is designed to help young people who have never studied painting to begin to appreciate pictorial art. I do not pretend that it can do much for the formation of taste, nor can it really teach anyone how to look at paintings, despite its title. What I hope it can do is to arouse in the reader some interest in pictures and perhaps provide him with food for thought about them.

I have always been against general books on art, and fundamentally I still am. It is therefore with great diffidence that I have written another book on the subject, but I have done so because I can remember how much certain books of this type aided me to acquire the little knowledge and the small degree of appreciation of art which I have today. They helped me because they were written in non-technical language and because they gave a simple explanation of the few elements of art which can be put into words; and none of them confused me by trying to describe that which cannot be described, namely, the process of creation.

I believe that studies on art fall naturally into two categories, the first dealing with external factors, such as construction, colour, volumes, etc., which can be explained and should be done so as simply as possible. Artistic sense and aesthetic value come in the second category, and can only be adequately expounded by the artists themselves and through their works.

Although I have written a general book on painting, I believe that every great picture deserves a whole book to itself, and I hope that increased interest in art will soon make this necessary. This book is only for young people and those adults who, without having studied art, have yet a genuine interest in it and want some help, expressed in simple language, to develop their interest. I hope that this little book will, in however small a degree, supply their need.

PART I

The Elements of a Picture

The elements of a painting and their significance

Most people have looked at paintings but not everyone who has looked at a painting has seen it. To have seen a painting means to have grasped and appreciated all the diverse qualities, aesthetic and technical, the picture on the canvas contains; that is, to have noted the construction, the disposition of volumes, of light and shade, and also to have become aware of atmosphere, colour, values, and so on. To understand what these various pictorial elements mean, one must first understand what each means separately and then see how all combine to form a painting. The finished picture can be compared to a man who is a combination of so many pounds of bone and flesh, so many pints of blood, so many ounces of acid. An amalgamation of these elements makes a man. Yet no one, knowing these facts alone about a human being, would claim to understand what a man is. The same applies to anyone knowing only the meaning and inter-relation of the elements of art.

For while this knowledge would help him to see how a picture is drawn and painted and put together, it will not give him the key to the inner meaning of the picture. To understand the inner meaning of a picture, that is, what the painter wishes to express in it, depends on either artistic intuition or on a very long experience in looking critically at pictures, and more often than not, on both. There is no formula which, when learnt and applied, can take one to the core of this understanding, but it is possible to elucidate certain points which can help those interested in art to attain some degree of art appreciation.

The elements of a picture, such as balance, atmosphere, perspective, light and shade, composition, drawing and painting, spring from one parent quality in the artist, namely, his artistic sense. It is not within the scope of this book to try to explain the meaning of this term, for this would involve a discussion on

9

aesthetics. However, the reader must accept the fact that artistic sense, more than any other single quality, is needed for the harmonious arrangement of all these elements into a whole, that is, into a picture.

The subject

The closer the subject is to nature, the more easily understandable it becomes. The more remote it is, and therefore the further removed from ordinary daily experience, the less easy it is to be understood. For some time it has not been very fashionable to attach too much significance to the subject. This is chiefly due to a confusion of thought. For the artist, the subject is the medium through which he attempts to exteriorize some concept or emotion. But being a medium, it can only have the importance that a mere medium can have, and can be compared to telegraph wires in relation to the words they transmit, for without this medium, the artist could not transmit his message.

If a medium has to be used, what the medium is may be of no great significance. Great artists have expressed themselves through various mediums. For example, Rembrandt expressed himself in portraits, biblical scenes, and landscapes. However, it is in self-portraits that he attains his most profound self-expression. For the artist, the subject is all-important only when it becomes part of his personality and is therefore an obsession, and when it is the only medium he can use to express himself. After the victory of the French over Spain and after the atrocities committed by the soldiers, Goya's mind became troubled with horrible visions and dreams. In the latter part of his life, he could only express himself by reproducing these visions, and the drawings which in his younger days were only excellent caricatures became charged with horror and obscenity. In his case, the subject had become part of his personality and because of that, all important.

The subject of a representational picture is self-evident, but a cubist picture, where the representational element is distorted, or an abstract picture which is not representational, has nevertheless a subject. But as a general principle, the qualities transmitted by this kind of subject have an intellectual rather than an emotional impact. Picasso expressed himself alike in representational, cubist and abstract forms.

While the subject is for the painter a mode of transmission, it is for the spectator a mode of reception. He is at first attracted to the subject because it stirs a certain feeling in him. It may be because of a pleasurable association or because it appeals to his imagination. A representational subject of a dramatic scene, like the

10

'Radeau de la Méduse', by Géricault, appeals mostly to emotion. An abstract composition by Braque or Picasso may appeal to the intellect. The importance of the subject seems therefore to be the first link between artist and onlooker. *Not* to attach importance to the subject should mean *not* to attempt to judge the qualities of the picture through the subject alone, but it does not mean that one should not be attracted by it. It must be remembered that the qualities of a work of art are independent of the medium through which they are transmitted.

The centre of interest

The centre of interest of a picture is the area where the principal action takes place and for this reason it is the part of the picture towards which the painter wants to attract our attention. For the artist, the choice of the centre of interest, is one of the most important elements of construction. Most representational painting, especially of the pre-impressionistic period, that is, painting representing life as we see it, has a definite centre of interest to which the eye of the onlooker should be instinctively drawn. The old masters more often than not confined their centres of interest within an imaginary line called by the French 'the arabesque', and composed their pictures so that this arabesque itself should become not only apparent, but also harmonious. The impressionists, who tried to depict nature in all its aspects, did not compose their forms so that they should fit into a preconceived outline, but followed the natural lines of landscape. However, it is probable that when choosing a vantage point for their easel, they selected it, not only with an eye to the harmonious whole but also with a pleasing 'arabesque' in mind.

In 'The Death of Procris', by Piero di Cosimo, the delineation, or arabesque, begins at the back of the faun and ends on the back of the dog who is watching Procris die. The centre of interest is within this line, for the action taking place between these two figures is the main action. The animals in the background and the beach itself do not directly participate in the drama of the painting and are therefore outside the centre of interest.

Volumes and masses

The words 'volume' and 'mass' when used in art criticism describe the visual effect of the properties these terms indicate in nature. In nature, a green tree that forms a mass on the sky, is a mass of green. The same tree can also be a volume for it can appear to us as a volume, that is, to have bulk. The same painting can be, and indeed often has been, treated both in masses and volumes.

In 'The Meninas' by Velasquez (in Madrid) the dog lying on the floor is treated as a volume, for he appears to be 'standing out' from the first plane. The other figures are treated as 'masses', especially the princess's dress, for it appears to be relegated more to the background than to project from it. Volumes or masses can be of different values, depending on the intensity of their colour, and the light falling upon them; for instance, the black of the dress of the lady-in-waiting kneeling in front of the Infanta is of a different value or intensity to the black suit of the painter, representing Velasquez himself.

Distribution of values

'Values' is the term used to describe the relation of different parts of a picture to the distribution of light. This distribution does not take the actual colour into account but only its intensity. Two planes of blue juxtaposed can be of two different values. Take, for instance, 'A Lady Standing at the Virginals' by Vermeer. Vermeer distributed his values by manipulating light through his masses and volumes. Thus, the window is a light plane from which the light is led into the room. It is then led by means of the wall, into a plane—the upper part of the lady's skirt—which it lightens. Above the skirt is a dark shawl, and under it a darker patch of the skirt, which is in shadow. At the end of the virginal is a picture which is in the light. The surface of the wall is broken by two pictures, on one of which the sun falls, while the other is in the shade. The face is divided into light and dark planes, as is the floor. This manner not only breaks up the monotony but gives a dramatic quality to a very quiet subject. Vermeer has not treated the light of the sun coming through the window in an entirely naturalistic way, but has arranged it, to suit his own purpose, in a somewhat arbitrary manner so as to be able to dispose his values in contrast to each other. Every painter has his own way of distributing values, and also his own preferences as to the extent to which he manipulates them. For instance, Manet in his 'Déjeuner sur l'herbe' represented the flesh of his central nude as one flat surface on which the rays of light have almost no play. The effect of this figure is one of opaqueness as opposed to the lustrous quality of the figure of 'A Lady Standing at the Virginals'. The treatment of the 'Déjeuner sur l'herbe' by Manet, is often referred to as 'flat treatment'.

Brushwork

'Brushwork' is the manner in which the painter applies the paint on the canvas. It is determined by the rhythmic movement of the artist's hand in using the brush. Every painter has his own 'touch' and he can be recognized through it as any other person is by his handwriting. Brushwork in painting is very much influenced by the temperament of the painter. Consider, for instance, two paintings, one by Seurat and the other by Van Gogh. One can see a great difference between the systematic touch of the pointillist, Georges Seurat, in 'La femme se poudrant', at the Courtauld Collection, and the wide criss-cross of Van Gogh's brushwork in his famous, 'Yellow Chair'. Although Van Gogh's touch repeats itself in most of his later pictures, it has not the systematic regularity of Seurat's touch. Seurat's method of applying pigment was part of the technique known as 'pointillism' evolved by him, while Van Gogh's style of putting paint on his canvas was his own personal manner of expressing himself. While both manners were individual, one was spontaneous and the other part of a system.

Different kinds of brushwork, that is, the various ways of applying paint, have been used by Renaissance and post-Renaissance painters to give an idea of weight. Celestial creatures like angels, and Our Lord Himself, were often painted with a lighter touch than terrestrial figures. In the painting of 'The Entombment of the Count of Orgaz' by El Greco, the celestial figures seem lighter in texture than the terrestrial figures, this effect being achieved through the difference of touch and of the thickness of the 'impasto'.

The touch is not always the impact of the brush on the canvas. Certain painters use the knife, while others, at some stage of the painting, even use their fingers. Painters who make use of the knife, use a heavier 'impasto'. 'Impasto' can be of thicker or thinner paste. Oil today is probably the most popular of all mediums. However, up to the thirteenth century, most paintings were painted in tempera, that is, with colours mixed with the white of an egg. Watercolour is of a lighter texture than oil. It has often been used by modern painters with great success. The water-colours of Cézanne are distinguishable from those of Constable, not only because of their very great difference in feeling and form, but also by their touch, or brushwork.

Passages and contours

A *passage** in painting is the meeting-point of two planes and the point at which

* The French term *passage* is retained as being more economical in expression and accurate in description than any English equivalent.

the painter's brush leads from one plane to another. A human face, although of the same texture throughout, is a rounded object which recedes in parts and protrudes in others. There are, for instance, many intermediary recessive planes between the nose and the ears. These planes are distinguished from each other by means of light and shade, that is, by the extent to which the sun is reflected in them. The places where these facets meet and dissolve into one another may be called transitions or *passages*. In Van Eyck's 'Portrait of a Man' the transitions are smooth, for they blend into one another. In Paul Cézanne's portrait of 'A Gardener' in the Tate Gallery, actual *passages* are rendered in a sharper manner so that the face and figure are divided into sections, and indeed this is true of the whole picture.

The 'contour' is a delineation of figures or objects within a picture. A contour can be sharp or soft. In 'Woman in a White Head-dress' by Van Eyck, it is obvious that the material of the head-dress seems as thin and sharp as a piece of paper, while the contour of the face is softer and rounder, thus rendering in a naturalistic manner the recession of the cheek towards the background. Many post-impressionist painters, like Van Gogh and Gauguin for example, sharpened their contours even when these delineated a face. In the case of Van Gogh, this was partly due to his desire to emphasize his liberation from the Renaissance painters and partly—especially in his later period—to the very vivid and tempestuous way in which he interpreted the world about him.

Solidity

A figure or an object in a painting is called 'solid' when it suggests weight. A figure is also called 'solid' when it seems to weigh upon the surface it stands on. If 'The Entombment' by Michelangelo is closely examined, it will be seen that the feet of the figure on the left make an impact on the ground, but the feet of Christ, His body being carried, make no such impact. The solidity of this picture is, therefore, rendered by the excellent drawing of the muscles and the contours of the feet. On close examination, one can see that the lines delineating the standing feet are firmer than those delineating the feet which are being carried. Although solidity and tactile quality are not the same thing, both are sculptural in origin. In a painting by a sculptor, although the figures are only shown two-dimensionally, their volume and solidity can normally be felt. One could imagine these figures outside their background and frame as a group of statuary. The artist has no doubt conceived them as being three-dimensional and therefore the colour and background were possibly only of incidental importance. Michelangelo lived at the height of the Renaissance and, therefore, of naturalism. No one, before or after him, rendered the human form with such three-dimensional perfection.

Atmosphere

There are two meanings to the word 'atmosphere' in painting. The wider meaning is the general feeling the whole composition gives to the onlooker. A painting can, for instance, have a romantic atmosphere, such as in a landscape by Claude, or a classical atmosphere, as in a painting by Poussin. The narrower meaning of the term describes the feeling the onlooker has of air circulating between the figures and objects represented, as it does in nature. In this painting by Turner, one feels that air moves among the trees and separates them from each other. This is achieved by the skill with which the painter renders not only distances, but also the airy space between them.

Perspective

'Perspective' in painting means the apparent nearness or distance of various objects on the same canvas. It is shown primarily by the size of the object, but it is also rendered by their position on the canvas. The way in which perspective is handled can make the world appear either infinite or as small as a matchbox. In 'Off Valparaiso' by Whistler, the ships recede into the distance to such an extent that the onlooker feels that he can follow their journey beyond the line of the horizon. In Van Gogh's 'Chair' there is also perspective, but in this case it represents only the very short distance which separates the edge of the seat from the back of the chair, and from the room in which it stands. Whistler had to graduate his tones to mark the distance between the boats and to lead the eye towards the horizon; Van Gogh had to place the chair within the room. The chair, being one solid object, its perspective is contained within its own shape, but also in its relationship to the space outside it. While Whistler had to show perspective by the use of atmosphere circulating between the boats, such treatment was necessary to Van Gogh in this particular painting only in a minor degree; in other words, although it still demanded a sense of perspective, the emphasis was not on this particular quality.

Perspective, which seems to us an integral aspect of a representational painting or drawing, was of little account before the fifteenth century when the great

Florentine architect, Brunelleschi, developed a system by which the 'vanishing point' of a picture could be mathematically arrived at.

This mathematical procedure was called 'Construzione Legittima' (legitimate construction). The height of the vanishing point was determined by the height of a man standing in front of the picture. Through joining the vanishing point by vertical lines to an imaginary line at the base of the picture and the same vanishing point to a point of vision outside the picture (the distance of this point of vision had to be calculated) a geometrical pattern was created which served as a skeleton for the depicting of perspective. Paolo Uccello, the Florentine painter of the 'Rout of San Romano' in the National Gallery, made a life study of perspective. His 'San Romano' is a well-known example of the application of perspective to painting.

Simplification

'Simplification' is the omission of one or more details in order to make the whole more harmonious or dramatic. Just as Constable does not paint every leaf of a tree, Picasso does not draw every line of the body. There are many more lines in the body of a horse than there are in the drawing by Picasso of 'A horse and a boy' at the Tate Gallery. He has sacrificed certain elements for the harmony of the whole. There is no rule for the amount of detail a painter may sacrifice. It must be left to his discrimination, and the success or failure of the result can only be judged by himself and those who understand his painting. However, most great painters aim at 'economy', which is a quality achieved through a discerning simplification. Meissonier in France and Copley in England rarely omitted details. Their painting seems lifeless not because of the wealth of these details but because the importance they gave to detail is much too great compared to the importance they gave to the whole. The early Flemish painters omitted no details, and this is true also of 'Le Douanier' Rousseau, and yet their paintings are alive because, however many details they included, they subordinated them to the harmony of the whole. The present tendency of some modern painters is to omit as many as possible of the details which do not seem to be essential. Others, on the contrary, seem to multiply them, yet keep very much in mind the necessity of subordinating them to the main features.

Light and shade

Light and shade technique in painting is the manner of rendering contrasts of light and dark. The term can also be applied to drawing. To shade a drawing is to darken certain parts of it so as to suggest the absence of the sun's reflection. Leonardo da Vinci at the height of the Renaissance, and later Correggio, developed the technique of light and shade and brought it into fashion. In 'Mercury instructing Cupid before Venus', by Correggio, at the National Gallery, the treatment is based on the contrast between the luminous flesh of the Venus, the darker tone of Mercury's and the Cupid's bodies and the intense dark of the foliage. The emphasis in contrast has the effect of giving the picture a sense of romanticism and mystery. This technique has been called 'sfumato'. Although it is generally designed to enhance the poetry and sentimentality of the subject, Rembrandt made use of it in his masterpieces, which are quite untouched with sentimentality.

To what extent a skilful arrangement of light has been responsible for the emotional depth of his self-portrait it is difficult to say, for greatness of Rembrandt's kind cannot be attributed to skill, or indeed to any superficial quality. However, the light on the face dissolving into deep shadows round the mouth, the dark background lightened round the head like a very faint halo, both contribute an unearthly quality to the portrait, an effect which Correggio never achieved nor probably had it in him to achieve. With seventeenth century painters such as Salvator Rosa, the abuse of this treatment of light and shade led to a reaction which can be seen in later schools, especially in the impressionist school.

One must be very careful not to confuse 'distribution of values' and 'light and shade technique', although both are instrumental in depicting light. For while 'distribution of values', is merely a notation of passages of light on a surface, 'light and shade technique', is designed to produce a definite effect.

Composition

Composition is the most important task of the painter and the ability to accomplish it gives both the artist and the spectator, more than any other special quality, a sense of fulfilment and well-being. Composition means the arranging of all the elements of the design, the figures or objects, in a manner which makes the picture a harmonious and satisfactory whole. This harmony is arrived at by disposing volumes and masses in the right relation to each other and therefore with the necessary equilibrium to please our sense of order and balance. How, in fact, do we judge a picture as far as composition is concerned? We judge it by the relationship that every part bears to the whole. Painters, in composing their

B

pictures, are faced with two distinct tasks. One, to relate the size of the canvas to the natural space in front of them. Two, to design their figures or objects to fit harmoniously into this space so that these figures should bear the right relationship, not only to each other within this space, but also to the space itself.

The two following concepts are often confused—proportion and symmetry. Both exist in nature. For instance, man is symmetrical because one side of his body is equal to the other. He is proportionate because his head has right relationship in size to his torso, and his torso to his limbs. Symmetry is law, proportion is changeable to a certain degree. For these reasons, the painter has the right to create his own proportions, and all that can be asked of him is harmony, which means that his ideas of proportion must appeal to our natural and innate desire for balance.

Every painter has his own mode of composition. Most painters have also their own devices which help them to keep to their composition. For instance, Poussin placed trees and buildings to act as 'verticals' in his pictures. These verticals, united to the horizontals, represented by land, or any plane surface, formed right angles at given distances from each other. Once this structure of right angles was achieved, figures and objects fell easily into the desired position. Owing to his rigid composition, his paintings, if somewhat stiff and conventional at times, never lack proportion.

Composition does not only apply to form but also to colour. Take, for instance, the 'Nativity' of Piero della Francesca, perhaps one of the greatest painters of the Renaissance. There are four distinct elements, or groups, in the design: the Angels, the Virgin, the Shepherd and St Joseph and the Christ Child lying on the ground. All the groups or figures are subordinated to the infant Christ lying on a blue cloth in the foreground. Although all Piero's figures seem to be unaware of the sanctity of the situation, the spectator's eye is immediately attracted to the infant Christ. This is because Piero placed him not only in the centre of the composition but also on the first plane. The cloak on which he lies is of a more intense blue than any other blue in the picture and only shares its intensity with the cloak of the Virgin, which is also in the foreground. The colours of the rest of the figures diminish in intensity as the eye is led inward. With regard to the arrangement of the various elements of the painting, it will be seen that the centre of interest of this picture is framed by the shed, which is remarkable in its square simplicity. Mid-height, on both sides of the shed, the composition continues, on the left by showing a glimpse of the Umbrian landscape and on the right by the introduction of a church. Both these parts of the composition seem to pick up the squareness of the shed. A black bird sits on one side of the shed. A dark wooden beam comes down from the roof, while the beam on the other side is unnoticeable because of its merging into the background. Although the bird and the beam are not symmetrical they give a sense of balance. All the elements of this composition are no doubt designed to give weight to the base and a feeling of lightness towards the top, thus giving the picture an impression of firmness and, at the same time, of surging upwards.

Paul Cézanne's method of composition was to break up the objects and figures he saw into cones and squares. The impression this gives is that of solidity within the specific object, which is a different kind of solidity from the sculptural solidity due to the pressure of a body on the ground. Cézanne's art has been instrumental in creating a new form of vision, which has led to an entirely new mode of representation.

The composition, or structure, of a painting need not be immediately apparent. It must, however, be present. Its presence must be felt like the underlying bone structure of a face, or the skeleton within the body. Without this a painting has a shapeless and 'fluffy' aspect which will fail to satisfy most people.

Drawing

Drawing cannot be separated from painting in a picture for each is a part of the other. A painter can draw with a pencil or brush, with a knife, or even with his fingers. Whatever the medium, he still draws. There are black and white paintings, for example, those of Mantegna, and those by Buffet, a modern young French painter who, up till recently, has scorned colour. A painter, however, does not usually draw his contours, then paint the colour inside them. When he draws his sketch, he has already in mind the distribution of volumes, masses, and also of colour. It is, however, very often through the drawing that one can judge of the sensitiveness of the painter. Many painters have left drawings and sketches which are unfortunately too rarely shown to the public.

The drawing of a painter is easily recognizable by the diversity of its lines. Thin and thick lines contrast with each other just as light and shade contrast in a painting. This happens because a painter can often visualize his paintings simultaneously in design and colour. Lines in his mind often stand for the intensity of colours, and their weight, or delicacy, suggest the degree of this intensity. The drawings of Rembrandt with their criss-cross of minute lines are typically a painter's drawings, which however does not in the least detract from their superb quality. Picasso, who, in some of his drawings, conducts his unfaltering line from the beginning of the form to its end, is a brilliant draughtsman as well as a painter. His lines are not drawn with the only ultimate end of appearing as pictures. Paul Klee, who likewise was both draughtsman and painter, that is, who did not only draw as a prelude to painting, believed in the power of the line to evoke movement and speed. There are many examples in his work of broken lines conveying the impression of atmosphere passing through them. One cannot decide arbitrarily whether an artist is primarily a draughtsman. It is only after having studied very many of his drawings that an opinion can be arrived at.

Sculptors' drawings are again very individual, and they are often quite different from painters' drawings. In Michelangelo's anatomical drawings, it can be clearly seen how preoccupied he was with the problems of sculptural or three-dimensional form. The way he ties the foot to the ankle so as to give all the ligaments the shape necessary for their true functioning is indeed the treatment of a sculptor. The same can be seen in Rodin's drawings. By and large, the difference between a painter's and a sculptor's drawing is that the painter's is less solid, its line being often broken and of unequal weight, while the sculptor's lines are firmer, and less often interrupted. The same may apply to painters who are also draughtsmen for drawing's sake.

Colour and half-tones

Colour has been left to the end of this chapter as it is the most complex but also, to my mind, the most external element of painting. One can, for instance, imagine a colourless world, a world in black and white as in a photograph (black and white not being colours). One can also imagine a world of mists or fluids, yet one cannot imagine an entirely shapeless world, for even mists and fluids assume some kind of form, however indefinite.

When we look at a rainbow, we see clearly three colours. Then, looking more attentively, we see three other colours. We see, therefore, six colours in all—violet, blue, green, yellow, orange, red. Three—red, blue and yellow, are primary colours. The others are formed by the mingling of two primary colours. In theory, the painter uses the colours of the spectrum, which is the scientific name for the six colours of the rainbow. In practice, he uses many more colours, or rather shades of colour. For red can be more or less red, blue can be more or less blue. To achieve this object, the painter has either to mix colours on his palette or juxtapose his colours on the canvas itself. A colourist is a painter who, by mixing his colours very skilfully, can achieve greater subtlety of shades.

Rembrandt, for instance, although his paintings seem to us dark-toned and even monochrome in general effect, is, nevertheless, one of the greatest colourists, for his use of colour is not only an essential part of his painting, but it also belongs intrinsically to the way in which he conceived his paintings, that is, they were conceived as compositions, but also as paintings. A striking example of this aspect of Rembrandt's genius may be seen in the subtlety of the colours of the dress, hands, face and background, and especially in the gradations of white, in his portrait of Marghareta Tripp. There is no absolute white in the composition, as nothing is absolutely white in nature, but the impression of whiteness is accentuated or diminished here by a subtle juxtaposition of shades.

There are many ways of applying colour. The primitives who used tempera achieved on the whole a purer effect than painters in oil. This was because tempera, as a medium, does not mix as well as oil and the pigments had to be applied pure. Even after the advent of oil-painting in Italy some painters, such as Piero della Francesca, retained their chromatic purity even while painting in oil.

A painter may use more than one coat of paint to achieve his particular effect. Poussin, for instance, used red as a base, then painted other colours on this red. This use of colour produced the desired effect, that is, it gave a warm internal glow to his figures independently of the external light. To achieve his purpose of light and dark planes, which make his figures appear to be lit by a ghostly gleam, El Greco used a grey base on which he applied very thin coats of colour so that the base shows through in places. The impressionist movement was in truth a revolt against the prevailing use of colour rather than a rebellion over form. To preserve purity of tint and yet to remain akin to nature they juxtaposed colours on the canvas in such a manner that the colours should mix in the eye when looked at from a certain distance. From this technique was developed another method of applying colour which is known as 'pointillism'. Pointillism consists in decomposing colour into its component parts, which are expressed in points of pure colour on the canvas, their juxtaposition bringing about the desired combination in the spectator's eye. This method sprang from the same source as impressionism and is in fact the systematization of the impressionistic method. It was also a reaction against the liberties taken by the impressionists at their most extreme. The inventor and, indeed, the father, of the method called 'pointillism' was Georges Seurat, who was followed by his pupils Signac, Cross and Luce.

With the cubist movement, which aimed at representing the world as a world of cubes, that is, at transforming it from organic into inorganic matter, the use of colour was very much reduced by many artists. Grey-browns, considered by some as a symbol for cerebral matter (which is commonly called 'grey-matter') replaced the colour discoveries of the impressionists. This attitude was by no means universal, however, for contemporary with the cubists and their chromatic sobriety were the Fauves, who indulged in an orgy of colour. It is interesting to note the strange similarity of tone between Rembrandt's colouring and that of the cubists. Rembrandt was the painter of the 'soul' while the cubists were painters of the 'intellect'. Both methods seem to reject the full-bloodedness and exaggeration to which abuse and crudeness of colour can lead.

The *local colour* of an object is the colour proper to the object, as, for instance, the green of a leaf. Every object has its local colour. It is the colour that serves as foundation for the painter's light and shade technique and for the distribution of values.

The *dominant colour* is the colour that is most prevalent in a painting. Great painters of the Renaissance and of the seventeenth and eighteenth centuries were always economical in the number of colours they used. For instance, there is always one dominant colour in Rubens's paintings. While he was particularly fond of using both red and blue, it is the red that is more often than not predominant. All the other colours are subordinate to this colour.

There are in painting *warm* and *cold tonalities*. Every direct ray of the sun falling on an object will automatically give it a warm gleam, while, on the other hand, its shadows will have a cold tonality. The converse is also true. When indirect light falls on an object, the effect is often one of coldness, but the shadows will have warm tonalities. This means that any colour can, according to the light, appear cold or warm. But whether it is warm, and the degree of its warmth or coldness, depends on whether it is lit directly or indirectly. In the portraits of Rembrandt, for instance, the salient parts such as nose and brow, are of a cold tonality, but only in relation to the tone of the local colour.

A *half-tone* is formed by the light that falls on an object and modifies its tonality. There are two kinds of half-tones; the half-tone which is part of the local colour of the object, that is, for instance a patch of dark-blue on a blue coat, and the half-tone which marks the passage between light and shade. This latter half-tone would be of a complementary colour to the local colour, that is, green in the case of red. Half-tones are also used to indicate a *passage* from one plane to another or from one object to another.

It must be emphasised that *absolute* white and black do not exist in nature; even snow is not absolutely white; they are however used in painting to darken or lighten an object. Grey, which is a composite of black and white, is the colour of clouds and like clouds can have a warm or cold tonality depending on whether or not the sun shines through them, or lights them. Grey can therefore be altered, that is, become a mixture of colours. El Greco's greys were the result of a combination of green, black and yellow. The subtlety with which he mixed his colours made him the great colourist he was.

The Italian painters of the latter part of the Renaissance and the Dutch painters used an excess of black and dark brown in order to give their pictures drama, mystery and romantic atmosphere. The revolt against black, came from the impressionist school.

PART II

Representational Painting

The portrait

A portrait is a drawing or painting, the purpose of which is to bear a resemblance to a model. However, artistically speaking, the outer resemblance to the sitter is by no means the only, or even the most important, element in a portrait. A portrait is subject to the same artistic requisites as any other painting, and if it evades them and concentrates solely on resemblance to the sitter, the result may be a portrait in the strict sense of the term, but it will not be a work of art. What makes a portrait a work of art? Apart from the other qualities already discussed, such as right distribution of masses, values, etc., it becomes a work of art when the painter can enter into the personality of the sitter and can reveal his inner self on the canvas. Yet it is not only the sitter's inner self that he shows but also his *own* inner self. The portrait must become, in fact, the artist's interpretation of the model and in this interpretation the painter must exercise his own inner artistic sense.

Holbein, who was one of the greatest portraitists of all time, understood the inner personality of his sitters to such an extent that not only did he never forget a face, but he also could fix on his paper their most fleeting and intimate expressions long after he had ceased to be in contact with them. There is a great difference between the portraits by Clouet, however excellent, and those by Holbein. While Clouet draws with the usual French 'finesse' the features of the courtiers of Francis II, Holbein puts into his portraits the exact touch that makes a face what it is, that is, the mirror of the inner self. He therefore transcends the art of portrait painting and unites both outer and inner resemblance.

Not many major artists of today choose to paint portraits. This may be because portrait-painting demands a close communication between sitter and painter; not only much time, but also a special effort of concentration, must be given to it. This no doubt interferes with the freedom that contemporary painters

The Leaping Horse by Constable.   *Royal Academy*
(See page 25)

consider to be their privilege. In the nineteenth century, there were, however, great portraits painted by Toulouse-Lautrec, Whistler, Sargent, and in the twentieth century, portraits by Picasso rank among the best.

The landscape

It is only comparatively recently that landscape painting achieved the importance it has today. Up to the time of the Renaissance the conception of landscapes in painting was idealistic and imaginary and during the greater part of the Renaissance it served as background for the action of the picture. Patinir, a Flemish painter, was the first artist to paint landscape for its own sake, but it was still an imaginary form of landscape, that is, divorced from reality. The Dutch School of the seventeenth century specialized in landscape, but apart from Ruysdael, Hobbema, and Philip de Coninck, their landscapes had a tendency to be idealized and mannerist. The Flemish Rubens' landscapes, however, were indeed in harmony with his genius. Later, in England, Constable showed the way to a new form of landscape painting. His approach to nature was one of love and humility. The sky was perhaps one of the most important elements in his pictures. He can be considered the first and perhaps one of the greatest of the impressionists, although this term was not invented until long after his death.

The impressionists made landscape the principal vehicle for expounding their theories and technique, and it is for this reason that there are so many of this period. The birth of impressionism took place in France in 1870, on the banks of the Seine and the Oise. It was the play of light on the water which gave the artists the first conceptions of their whole subsequent technique. The treatment they applied to water, had, for the sake of balance, to be applied also to houses, trees, etc. Out of nature they took only one element, that is, light; light which is not the object itself, but only 'colours' the object. What the impressionist painted was in fact 'the appearance of reality'. One of the most important contributions of the impressionists to art was the brightening of painting by banishing black from their palettes, which, they said, did not exist in nature. They had discovered that two tones of colour placed next to one another produced a lighter effect when seen at a distance than colours mixed in the usual way on the palette, and they therefore applied this principle to their compositions. Manet, Pissaro, Renoir, but especially Monet, were the founders of this technique. Monet, in his latest pictures, carried it to extremes by 'lightening' his pictures until the forms depicted in them became hardly visible. This period is, in the opinion of many enlightened critics, perhaps his best. But as in most theories, the impressionistic theory had in it the seed of its own destruction.

The fundamental revolt of the impressionists was against the 'grand and majestic' landscape. Going about the country with their easels, they painted simple country scenes, fields and rivers. They did not wish to preach nor to depict 'peasant life'. They just wanted to illustrate their theories in showing life as it really was. This departure was, in fact, a 'bourgeois' revival. Did the impressionists consciously compose their pictures? Properly speaking they did not; they placed themselves in front of a view and painted what they saw. If they did not compose consciously, they may have done so subconsciously, for most paintings have in them an element of composition. They did so, no doubt, by setting their easel in the right position for this purpose and by choosing the moment when the distribution of light was suitable.

The requisites of landscape painting are similar to those of other paintings and one of the fundamental laws is a harmonious relationship between the component parts of the design and their harmonious relationship to the whole. Ideally, the onlooker should become part of the landscape and the landscape should symbolize for him at least one aspect of the world. Take, for instance, Hobbema's famous 'Avenue'. A man walks with his dog in the cool of the evening in a Dutch village. We know it is the evening because the action and every element of the picture makes us feel the mood of this evening hour, and through the feeling it evokes in us it achieves its purpose. In Cézanne's 'Mont St Victoire', the landscape depicting this particular part of sunny, dried-up Provence, symbolizes not only the whole of this province of France but also this particular aspect of the world, that is, dryness, heat, and summer. How do these pictures differ from 'The Angelus', by Millet? In 'The Angelus' two peasants bend their heads self-consciously while the bell is ringing. The picture is well-composed but the pose of the peasants in their made-up simplicity attempts to show the worth of peasant life—the honesty of labour. This picture tries to preach, and for this reason does not give the pure aesthetic pleasure that the others give. In the case of 'The Angelus' it is art subordinated to a moral meaning, while art should be a law unto itself, not infringing upon morality. The two other pictures deal in different ways with pure and simple aesthetics.

Still life
Still life is a painting of objects disposed in such a manner as to give an aesthetic

pleasure to the onlooker. A still life can be therefore more aptly called a composition than any other form of painting. More often than not it is 'composed' by the artist, not only mentally but also physically, before he attempts to paint the actual picture. It may not be an absolute necessity for the painter to compose his still lives beforehand, for sometimes nature forms them in a better order than the painter could do himself in any composition, however successful. It is, in almost all cases, a co-operation between the two: nature, in which accident prevails, and man, who imposes order. Aristotle said: 'Art completes what nature cannot bring itself to finish'—a thought which can be applied very appropriately to still life. Still life painting is a very important sub-division of the history of art, as it is possibly the precursor of the modern abstract movement. When we think of a still life we often imagine Dutch flowers or fruit which are so perfectly represented that we feel we could almost touch them. We also see mountains of food —lobsters, hares, fish or poultry—heaped up on a canvas. We are sometimes seized with revulsion. If we analyse this revulsion we find that it is because this super-abundance offends our sense of good taste. But if we look at a still life by Chardin, harmoniously composed, not only in form but also in colour, we get a feeling of tranquillity and happiness which we rarely find in any other subject.

The French have always had a natural bent towards still life, owing, no doubt, to their characteristic love of order and subtlety. Fantin Latour painted flowers and fruit with no less grace than Poussin his Muses. The still life paintings of Cézanne, especially those painted in watercolours, illustrate perhaps his genius best. This is probably because this particular mode of painting was more akin to his aesthetic sense than any other. His method of resolving the atmosphere and subject into squares and cones could not find a better medium than that of the still life. Such objects as bottles, plates, tables, devoid as they are of any life of their own (the French term 'nature morte' is singularly appropriate here) gave him a greater measure of freedom of expression than any other subject could bestow. For in a still life, the artist is freed from all outside influences due to the actual presence of a 'living' subject, whether man, animal or tree, for the fact of being 'alive' must have an effect, however small, on the artist himself. Picasso, Braque, Juan Gris, expressed themselves in still life more freely than in any other of their compositions. Although the choice of subjects in a still life by Braque or Picasso was often almost identical, and at one period their styles were very much alike, Picasso in his painting has great strength and a clear-cut quality, but Braque's main concern is finesse and taste. In his still life paintings, Braque gives us perhaps the greatest pleasure that we can derive from any such painting, if what we are looking for are balance and harmonious composition.

A still life should also convey a feeling of permanence, for the subject being motionless suggests changelessness and timelessness. The aesthetic dangers inherent in still life painting can be the opposite of those which disfigure portrait or landscape painting. In dealing with inanimate objects, some 'feeling' may be lost. Fantin Latour is a good example of this, for while his early works show a certain pungency, it is lost in his later pictures owing not only to his preoccupation with the smoothness of his treatment but also to his complete subjection to the object. Courbet's still life may owe some of its strange quality to the fact that he was a wild and disorderly human being; the stillness of the subject had, perhaps, the effect of curbing his turbulence and for this reason his still life work shows a combination of qualities which are necessary requirements of art—strength and sobriety.

Religious painting

A religious painting is one which depicts an aspect of religion, be it a representation of the Entombment, the Nativity, the martyrdom of saints or any subject which pertains to the Church. Many of the paintings by Italian masters which are to be seen today in museums have a religious scene for subject. The reason why religious subjects were so often chosen by these artists is obvious—the Catholic Church was not only a great power; it was also a rich and powerful patron and it used art to propagate the faith. A second reason was that the artists themselves were more under the influence of the Church than they are today. A third reason was that the clergy, and especially the priors, owing to their superior education, were aware of the necessity for beauty and felt the need to have their churches and convents adorned by the leading artists of the day. This only applies to painters in Catholic countries. For later painters in Protestant countries were influenced by the Reformation and the tenets of the Reformed faith did not encourage the depiction of religious subjects.

A religious picture, like every other painting, has to conform to the requisites of art. There is, however, another element that must be present in such works, namely, religious feeling. Many paintings of a religious subject lack religious feeling and this is why they do not stir us, in spite of their subject, as much as do those paintings which, in addition to it, are infused with religious feeling. To infuse religious feeling into a painting is to give the figures representing Christ,

28

the Madonna, or the saints, some intangible quality which expresses their divinity, their sainthood, that is, a quality which seems to show that although they are depicted as people, yet they are moved by different feelings from those which move ordinary human beings.

The expression of grief on the Madonna's face which appears in most paintings of the Crucifixion pertains to two levels of existence, the human and the divine. For the Madonna, although a woman, through being the Mother of Christ, is partly divine and partly human. If only the human quality were shown, she would be an ordinary mother weeping over her son; and if the divine quality alone were expressed, no grief could be shown, for grief is primarily a human emotion. It is the degree to which this suggestion of a divine quality can be depicted which, to my mind, makes a painting religious or non-religious in feeling. This quality must naturally be coloured by the personal conception of the painter. Piero della Francesca conveys this mystical quality by giving to the faces he paints a unique expression of unawareness. Their unawareness does not mean indifference, but rather a shifting of their attention and interest to beyond this world. It seems as if the real action were being enacted in some divine sphere, while the action in the painting is only a reflection of this other more important reality. For instance, in the artist's picture of Christ's baptism in the National Gallery, the figures seem entirely untouched by the importance of the action. The only reminder, apart from the two standing angels, of its profound religious significance lies in the Holy Ghost descending in the form of a dove over the head of Christ; the whiteness of the dove is perhaps slightly more intense than the white of the clouds. 'The Baptism of Christ', an early canvas by Piero della Francesca, is probably, of all the paintings in the National Gallery, the picture which produces in the spectator the most intense religious feeling—and it does this in spite of the 'unaware' expressions on the faces of the figures.

Mattias Grünewald had perhaps the very opposite religious approach to that of Piero della Francesca. This is seen clearly in his crucifixion on the altarpiece of Isenheim at Colmar. For while Piero's personages seem to be unaware of the drama of the subject, those of Grünewald seem to be entirely under the emotional spell. However, this awareness is solely directed towards one point of the action, that is, Christ dying on the Cross. Through the strength and humanity of her grief, Mary Magdalene is entirely unaware of anyone else or anything else around her. The quality of the divine is represented in the picture by the tension between the calm of the figure of Christ on the Cross, and the entirely human pathos of Mary Magdalene.

The apparent difference, therefore, between the religious qualities of these two painters are the following: while Grünewald's figures enact the drama within the picture, Piero della Francesca's figures seem moved by a drama which takes place outside the picture. These representations of what may be called 'the divine' in a painting are extreme examples of the form this quality can take. Many other great religious painters, such as Fra Angelico and Giovanni Bellini, have been able to infuse other religious qualities into their pictures without, however, such extreme emphasis upon either emotion or the apparent lack of it. The Spanish master, El Greco, imbues his pictures with a religious feeling not only through the expressions of ecstasy he gives to the faces of his saints and Madonnas, but also by making his celestial figures appear less solid than the bodies of other living beings. It must be remembered, however, that although religious subjects were very often chosen, the Renaissance period was not, properly speaking, a time of religious painting. The painters I have just described are perhaps the greatest of the religious painters, for they all infused religious feelings into their pictures. But they were in the minority. With the Counter-Reformation, most religious painting lost its only important significance, that is, religious feeling, and became representational painting depicting celestial figures.

Historical painting
From the period of the Renaissance, when the worship of man came to the fore, every prince and every general wanted to be shown engaged in the exercise of his calling. The artists often represented their friends and patrons, and sometimes themselves, as actors in an historical or even in a religious scene. Ghirlandaio portrayed the whole of elegant Florentine society in his pictures, even although most of them had a religious subject. Historical painting proper did not wane as religious painting did, but, on the contrary, came very much to the fore at the end of the eighteenth century, especially during the Napoleonic wars. At this period, painters interested in historical subjects could not fail to find interesting characters and situations to depict. Napoleon wished to be immortalized both as a general and an Emperor, and he employed the painter Baron Gros to show him in many aspects of his official life.

What constitutes an historical painting? It is, among other factors, a marriage between the scene and the characters within the scene, that is to say, it has two subjects. But as in any other painting, every idea should be subordinated to a central idea, which means that one of the two subjects should out-weigh the other in importance. In an historical painting, there is perforce a mixture of subjects, for there are *two* subjects of equal importance instead of one. They are of equal importance because they are so closely interrelated. A general is only important through his battles. Therefore, he must be accurately represented. The battle is important as it is the arena of the general's importance. Besides, accuracy of representation was often, in historical subjects, demanded of the artist by the patrons.

One subject should be subordinate to the other, but which of the two should be subordinate? There is, naturally, no general rule and every artist must follow his own feeling. Apart from this subjection of one theme to the other, the artist must infuse into his work, whatever the subject, his own aesthetic sense. An historical painting has therefore more problems to contend with than any other kind of painting, for it is a portrait within a portrait. An historical picture—like a sentence which contains a mixed metaphor—suffers from what can be termed overabundance. The painter of an historical scene, preoccupied as he is with his two subjects, may find it difficult to inject artistic sensibility into the picture. The result of this failing is often seen as an unnecessary wealth of detail, which takes away from the harmony of the whole. We cannot say of either Delacroix or Géricault that they are, properly speaking, 'historical painters'. While they often derived their subject from history, they felt free to depict this as they chose. 'Liberty leading the People', by Delacroix, represents the artist's idea of this historical event. The faces he depicted are the faces which he felt were appropriate to the event. They are 'archetypes' in a symbolical situation—the fight for Freedom. I do not mean by this that he used no actual models, but he exercised complete freedom in depicting them, and the whole of the conception was subordinated to his artistic sense. Likewise historical paintings by a Tintoretto or a Titian cannot be called historical painting in the strict sense of the term, for owing to the greatness of their conception they transcend the narrow field of historicism to become works of art. Uccello painted battle scenes, and although he no doubt represented with accuracy, yet it was not the subject, one feels, which chiefly interested him. In the 'Rout of San Romano' it was neither the expressions on the faces of the soldiers, nor the battle, which were all-important to him as a painter, but the concept of the whole scene and the problems of perspective it posed.

31

No great painter can be described as solely and purely an historical painter, for the great painter would never make the mistake of giving too much importance to the subject at the expense of his artistic sense, and thus he could never be classified in any narrow category.

Genre

Genre painting can be described as a form of historical painting, the difference being that while historical painting treats of great occasions, genre painting treats of intimate everyday subjects.

Like historical painting, it is bound to be an inferior form of painting through its obvious limitations. However, a genre subject will not necessarily mean a genre painting. When Rembrandt painted his 'Night Watch', he painted, properly speaking, a genre painting, as he represented watchmen and guards going about their usual duties. Nevertheless, this particular painting cannot be called a genre painting, nor Rembrandt 'a genre painter', for his genius transcends all styles and manners in art.

1. The Death of Procris by Piero di Cosimo. *National Gallery*

(See page 11)

C

2. The Meninas by Velasquez. *Prado Museum*
(*See page 12*)

3. A Lady Standing at the Virginals by Vermeer. *National Gallery*
(*See page 12*)

4. The Entombment by Michelangelo. *National Gallery*
(*See page 14*)

5. Nativity by Piero della Francesca. *National Gallery*
(*See page 18*)

6. The Baptism of Christ by Piero della Francesca.   *National Gallery*
(*See page 29*)

7. Self Portrait by Rembrandt. *National Gallery*
(*See page* 17)

8. Rout of San Romano by Uccello.   *National Gallery*
(*See page 16*)

9. The Avenue by Hobbema. *National Gallery*

(See page 26)

10. Off Valparaiso by Whistler.   *Tate Gallery*
(See page 15)

11. Liberty Leading the People by Delacroix. *Louvre*
(See page 31)

12. La Femme du Cirque by Rouault. *Private Collection*
(*See page 52*)

13. Gueridon, Verres, Tasses, Mandoline by Picasso. *Private Collection*
(*See page 42*)

14. Static, Dynamic, Contrasting by Paul Klee. *Private Collection*
(*See pages 20 and 51*)

15. Bouteille, Verre et Pipe by Braque.   *Private Collection*
(*See page 44*)

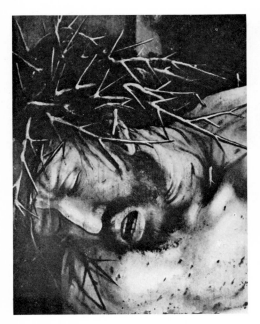

16. The Crucifixion by Mattias Grunewald
(*Colmar Museum*) with details of the head and
left arm of the figure of Christ.
(*See page 29*)

PART III

Manners of Painting

There are, very broadly speaking, three manners of painting: the original, the derivative and the imitative manners.

Original

One could say that a painting is original when, whatever its subject and treatment, it originated in the artist's mind. If one took this explanation literally, it would mean that no work of art could be original unless it showed an entirely new conception and form. Yet one cannot say that a representational work of art, that is, one showing human forms in a human situation, such for instance, as a nativity, need necessarily be non-original. Originality or non-originality must be a matter of degree. A crucifixion by El Greco is a good example of what is meant by degree in this context. This is a subject which has been used by many painters. Therefore, as a subject, it is not original. But El Greco's conception of the Crucifixion is entirely different from any other representation of the same theme. Not only is it different in technique but it is also different in treatment. The violence in El Greco's treatment of the scene is not only due to human grief, but also to the violence of nature. The depiction of the fury of the lightning that illuminates the body of Christ and the face of the Madonna is an original conception. The grouping of the figures, which seem drawn towards the sky, the elongation of their bodies which seems to express the tension between matter and spirituality are also original. The crucifixion by Grunewald, in which the grief of Mary Magdalene, however intense in appearance, is none the less of a human quality, has also great originality, but instead of the tension between two planes of experience, the tension it expresses is due to a violent but entirely human passion. The suggestion of the divine is concentrated around Christ's head, where the prismatic colours of the rainbow are shown with extreme brilliance. Both crucifixions are original conceptions of the same familiar theme.

33

D

Modern painters, and especially 'abstract' painters, tend perhaps more towards originality than the painters of previous schools. Picasso, in his painting, has probably shown more originality than any other artist. His originality is expressed in a constant invention of new forms and aspects of life. He can indeed, be called a creator. The danger of originality in art lies in seeking after it. It is a subtle quality which, if it is sought after may lose its virtue, for it may then be derived from the desire to be original and, in the result may lose originality. Although sincerity is the most important factor in originality, an artist can be sincere without necessarily being original.

Derivative

A derivative painting is a painting in which inspiration, or treatment, or both, are derived from an historical source or a sister art. The most usual form is illustration of an historical event. Ford Madox Brown's 'The Last Look at England', is derivative because it illustrates an episode in the lives of the emigrants. Likewise, illustrators of a book are derivative because they illustrate the incidents described in the book. Art does not only consist in visual art; the term includes also music, literature, poetry, drama, etc. Literature and poetry have often been inspired by historical events, and historical characters who have been heroic, tragic, romantic, poetic and a painter inspired by romantic events will express his romanticism by painting romantic characters in romantic scenes. He will be called a romantic painter, as, for instance, were Delacroix and Géricault, or a classical painter, as was Poussin. Raphael was inspired by classical Greece and therefore can in a sense be called derivative. Yet, however derivative these artists were in subject, and especially in mood, their personalities were so powerful that they could not fail to have a strong effect on their work in spite of this tendency. However classically inspired Poussin may have been, the influence of his own character is apparent even in the most classical example of his art. Poussin became derivative when he allowed his love for classicism to overwhelm his artistic sense and it is then that his pictures lose that degree of freedom which all great works of art must have.

Delacroix and Géricault, who both belong to the romantic period, were influenced by literary subjects, such as scenes of Arab life, and medieval themes. Their paintings are derived from them, but their personalities have such power that they break through this influence. Mantegna is perhaps one of the painters whose personality became with age more and more subjected to classicism.

While Raphael was a lover of ancient Greece, Mantegna was a lover of ancient Rome. All the attitudes of his figures are classically Roman. Yet even though he can be called derivative, this quality in him has originality, for it represents his personal, and therefore original, idea of classicism. There is however a difference between the first examples of originality, given above, that is, crucifixions by El Greco and Grünewald and the subjects chosen by Delacroix and Géricault. Between the ninth and seventeenth centuries, the Crucifixion became a theme so often represented that it ceased to be a subject and became a 'symbol'. Therefore originality could not be due to the choice of subject, but to its treatment. The same cannot be said of Géricault and Delacroix, nor of Raphael and Mantegna. Their subjects were not symbols in the sense in which the Crucifixion had become a symbol, but were dependent on their mood. Their choice was influenced by literature, poetry and history. It does not mean that these four great painters lacked greatness or even freedom of conception; it only means that they were influenced by other artistic factors. Derivativeness in art is naturally only a matter of degree. As all art issues from the human intellect and heart, both of which are obviously influenced by other artistic movements, it is bound to be, however slightly, derivative. Even abstract art is up to a point derivative, as it derives certain of its new forms from the constructionist world of today.

Imitative

Imitative art is imitation either of a painter's manner or of another painting. The painters who copy great masters in galleries are either imitators of manner or engaged in copying a painting. Imitation is sometimes conscious, sometimes subconscious. Copyists are conscious imitators, while the rigid followers of a particular school of painting are often subconscious imitators. We shall only deal with subconscious imitators, for copyists are not creative artists.

Every pupil is taught by a master, and he will imitate him up to a point. However, his own personality, if he has one, breaks through sooner or later. Most great masters who have worked in an atelier during their youth have had an imitative period. El Greco imitated Tintoretto until his arrival in Spain, yet there are few painters who became more original in style than El Greco.

Today, while the great masters of the past are universally acknowledged as being great, they are no longer imitated, nor is much art derived from their masterpieces. The same cannot be said of the impressionists, who still have many imitators. Cézanne, who was not properly speaking an impressionist, has perhaps been imitated more than any other painter. Picasso, Braque, Matisse and Rouault, who are undoubtedly at the pinnacle of modern art, cannot fail to find imitators at the present time.

A period in which only a few great painters emerge and remain so long to the fore is doubly dangerous, not only because of the monotony this produces, but because of its effect on taste, and fashion, which derives from taste. If painters are judged by whether they do or do not resemble Picasso, limits are set which result in the fettering of judgment and of artistic criticism. Ideally, artistic judgment should be free of all comparisons, but like all ideals, entire artistic freedom of judgment is hardly possible. Every painter, however great, can, in the course of his career, have been imitative, derivative and original at different periods and in varying degrees.

PART IV

From the Primitives to Modern Art

The changing forms of art

It is not the purpose of this book to write a history of art through the ages. I would, however, like to say what I feel about the process of change that has taken place during the last five hundred years in Western European art. Change in visual expression comes probably from two things—supply and demand, but it is difficult to say which comes first. From time to time a subconscious desire for new forms of aesthetic expression grows alongside what may be called 'official' art, that is, the established, traditional modes of art, and the need creates the supply. The converse can also be true. New forms of art may be created independently of any demand and the demand grows because the artistic world is ripe for innovation.

The last five hundred years, the period between the Middle Ages and the present day, have witnessed the following changes: from medieval art to Renaissance art; from Renaissance art to the forms of art known as genre and baroque; from baroque and genre art to impressionism; from impressionism to pointillism; from pointillism to cubist and abstract art. It is an error to think that modern art is essentially abstract. Many artists have returned to representational expression in their work. Nevertheless, it is a fact that the abstract movement, especially on the Continent, gathers strength and momentum yearly. What is particularly noticeable about these changes over the centuries in art and styles and motives? Chiefly that they are at very irregular intervals, and of varying importance. The lapse of time between impressionism and abstract art is barely twenty years, while the change from medieval to baroque art took at least two centuries to come about. The importance of these successive movements in art varies greatly. What is important in art? It is neither the subject depicted nor the manner in which the subject is shown on the canvas; it is the way in which the artist sees the world and expresses what he sees.

37

There have been two great changes in art: (1) primitive to the Renaissance; (2) representational to non-representational art, which to my mind began with the early forms of cubism. The changes in between, namely, from Renaissance to baroque and genre, were part of a normal process. The impressionist movement, which is considered by many to mark the transition from traditional to modern art, is not, in my opinion, the important break it is commonly believed to be. The impressionist revolt was probably mostly concerned with colour technique and choice of subject-matter. There is in the representational painting of the impressionists no fundamental alteration of the shape or form of the object or of human beings, such as took place later. The change to abstract painting, which, once initiated, developed very rapidly, was heralded by Cézanne, but only reached its real point of departure with early cubism.

Medieval art

If one examines the art of this whole period, namely, five hundred years, it will be observed that objects were not painted realistically in medieval times, as they were from the Renaissance onwards, for both medieval and abstract art represent man and nature in forms different from those the eye sees. Yet, although medieval and abstract representations seem to have a certain relationship, they spring from different sources. Both represent man and object other than we see them, but they do so for different reasons. The medieval world was a world of ideals as opposed to a world of scientific facts. Art was used in the service of the Christian Church, and it was Christian ideals that it tried to represent. Man was held to be a non-important being except for his relationship to God and it is therefore in this relationship that he was shown. What was the relationship of man to God? It can be defined as whether or not his actions were dedicated to the service of God. A man was not often represented as just a man, but either as a saint or a sinner. Hence, the hieratic gestures of the saints and the deformity and grimaces of sinners. In fact it was prayer, sin, and sanctity that were represented and not man himself. Sin and sanctity, are abstract notions, and thus medieval art has an abstract element in it.

Renaissance art

With the Greco-Roman excavations and particularly with the spread of the Sicilian-Greco-Roman culture which was revived in the reign of Frederick II of Hohenstaufen, classical beauty became the predominant preoccupation of artist

38

and painter alike and man was represented henceforth for his own sake. If many painters of the Renaissance kept their abstract qualities, that is, strove towards the abstract ideal and composed their pictures in a way which tends to abstraction, they did it against the popular movement and because it was for them an inner necessity. While it is true that the great majority of Renaissance paintings were of religious subjects, nevertheless the chief preoccupation of most painters of the time was to glorify man, and religious feeling entered into their conception as a secondary aim.

What is there in common between the abstract art of today and primitive art, and where does the difference lie? The point in common is that both medieval and abstract paintings do not glorify man but use the human form to transmit an idea. In other words, man's form is of secondary and not of primary importance. The difference lies in the fact that an aesthetic concept has been substituted for the concept of Deity in the ideas transmitted by modern artists. If these ideas are related to God at all, it is only in the sense of God being an aesthetic perfection.

Cubist art

If one wished to date the birth of cubist art, however approximately, it could be said that it began in 1909 when Picasso painted his 'Demoiselle d'Avignon'. The break seems to come, in fact, in the middle of the painting. On the left, the nudes are still almost representational, while the two figures on the right are already painted in a way that heralds a new kind of vision. For one can already discern in them a certain element of early cubism. Picasso, it is said, was at this time influenced by Negro art and traces of this influence can be seen in the faces of the two 'demoiselles'. Yet who can deny the right to innovators of being influenced? Very soon Picasso, Braque, and Juan Gris headed the short-lived but very significant cubist movement, which, followed as it was by the abstract movement proper, was instrumental in creating the new aesthetic values of today which are so incomprehensible to many people.

Abstract art

The term 'abstraction' can be understood quite simply. It is explained in philosophy by Plato. In art, it means the pictorial expression of nature by pictorial absolutes, such as squares, circles, cubes, curves and spirals. A square, or a circle, must each be perfection in itself. For one perfect circle cannot be more perfect than another circle, as both true circles must be perfect. When two circles are juxtaposed, they may mean mathematical perfection, but not necessarily an artistic achievement. Yet, abstract artists are also creators of artistic forms. They achieve this by the relationship of absolutes, that is, by composing these absolutes into a harmonious whole.

Although this book deals only with painting, it is difficult when writing of abstract art to separate it entirely from sculpture and architecture. Abstract art is mainly a play of shapes in space and it can therefore be best expressed in threes dimensional construction, for then, unhampered by colour and the limitation-imposed by canvas, it can more easily achieve the harmony and balance, which is its chief purpose. To the question, What is abstract art concerned with? it can be answered that it deals with the essence of the outer appearance of things and their arrangement into forms and planes, so as to fit into some general pattern.

Take, for example, a bottle standing on a table. While an expressionist will try to express what the bottle means to him, and in most cases will dramatize this meaning, the abstract painter will only deal with what he considers to be the essence of its shape, and will not concern himself with any inner meaning of the object. In this respect abstract art is not unlike Greek art of the great centuries, the period when its great beauty was achieved by concentration on the harmony of the outer form.

In language, the abstract means a departure from the concrete, and in art it denotes abandoning the conventional. But if it is to retain artistic quality, abstract art must develop, and it has its own quite definite conventions. To take abstraction to a further point is hindered by the limitations imposed by the canvas and the conventional shape of the frame, both of which act as a brake. The advantages of such a brake are debatable. However, an abstract picture, the frame of which follows the general rhythm of the line, is not necessarily an absurdity, for thus the design is helped to leave the narrow pictorial world and become a composition in space—which it is designed to be. However much we may be in disagreement with this new vision, it must be realized that we are part of, and live in, an abstract world.

Although Picasso can be called the father of the abstract school, abstract quality has always existed in art. What is the abstract quality of a painting? We can say a painting has an abstract quality when all its elements such as colour, composition, etc., can be decomposed into absolutes such as angles, triangles, etc., and when these absolutes are subordinated to the harmony of the whole composition. Piero della Francesca's paintings have an abstract quality, for his figures bear a mathe-

The Deposition by Ugolino Da Siena. *National Gallery*

(See page 41)

matical relationship to each other. If this relationship were disturbed, our sense of balance would, in turn, be disturbed, and one of the greatest elements of this painter's pictorial beauty would disappear. Every great painting has a quality of abstraction, and almost every great painter of the Renaissance sought for some form of abstraction. Uccello's researches on perspective are well known. When one says that the Renaissance painters were naturalistic, it is only a half-truth, for although they glorified natural beauty, they certainly searched for systems of design by following the laws by which absolute perfection might be attained. Subconsciously we look for an abstract quality in every representational painting.

However, one must not over-simplify the term 'abstract quality', for while regarded constructionally, it may mean reducing the composition to geometrical forms, it has still another meaning, which consists in abstracting from all the elements the one which constitutes the core of the picture and emphasizing its importance. Every picture is a combination in varying degrees of emotion and intellectual ideas, which must be subordinated to a central feeling, or concept. In the 'Deposition', by Ugolino da Siena (active between 1317 and 1327) the central idea of the picture is, to my mind, the expression of the Madonna's grief. The mood of the whole composition is subordinated to this feeling, and the impression the onlooker receives is that of sorrow. Grief is in itself an abstract concept, which in this picture is transmitted to us unmingled with any other emotion of a different nature. Yet if the construction of the picture is examined, it will be seen that it can be resolved into geometrical shapes. The whole group could be fitted into a semi-circle, the line of the back of the apostles being continued in the line of the back of Christ, and coming to an end with the end of the Holy Women's cloaks. One must not forget that art is man made and that the personality which feels the necessity of 'abstracting' will probably do it in concept as well as in construction.

Cubism may be regarded as a first step towards abstraction, for although in this method of painting, the subject, whether animate or inanimate, is decomposed into cubes, yet a definite link is usually kept with its real form. It is also called simultaneous vision as every part of the body is represented through cubes which are mathematically equal on all sides. Every facet can be imagined by reference to one of the sides of the cube.

The subject, thus decomposed, loses some of its relationship to nature, becoming instead related to 'absolutes'. Thus, the subject leaves the world of emotion for the world of the intellect because it is only mentally that one can equate each

F.

side of a cube. (I am only referring now to the mechanism of understanding a cubist composition, for it is obvious that finally the spectator must feel stirred both emotionally and intellectually.)

Picasso, who is one of the originators of cubism, seldom lost complete sight of nature, and if one looks attentively enough at one of his cubist pictures, the subject soon takes shape. It is in fact, a double artistic achievement, for it is both naturalistic and abstract. Great artists knew that to lose complete sight of nature was, however courageous a venture, yet fraught with danger, as it may lead to loss of all feeling. For this reason, an abstract or a cubist painting in which the parts bear neither a relationship to each other and to the whole, nor to nature, is often worse than a bad painting for it is devoid of both ugliness and beauty which are attributes of art. It fails, therefore, to become an artistic creation. The complete departure from the representational subject occurred only at a later period when cubes were 'flattened' into planes. This is the case to a large degree with abstract painting today.

The years 1906-1914

How did the world take to abstract art? Those who looked for pure emotional experience could not get used to the new images; those who believed that appreciation of art had to be partly intellectual welcomed it. It was mostly understood and liked by younger people, especially by musicians, and those who had had a philosophical training and therefore had developed a taste for 'abstract thinking'. Children seem to take to it at once. So as to understand how the present generation has been conditioned to abstract art, it is necessary to realize the significance in art of the period beginning about 1906, which reached full bloom just before the 1914 war. The centre of the movement was Paris. At this period the psychological methods of Sigmund Freud had already begun to influence the enlightened. It is impossible to say whether the works of the great psycho-analyst on Negro customs had a direct bearing upon the interest in African art, but it is a fact that entirely alien forms of beauty began to be represented.

Picasso's 'Negro Period' perhaps marks the appropriate starting point of the great decade. As I have said before, it is enough to look at the 'Demoiselles d'Avignon' to note the break between the old and new conceptions and also to see the beginnings of cubism. More or less at the same period a movement called *Der Blaue Reiter* came to the fore in Germany, of which Franz Marc and

Kandinsky were two of the most significant artists. Two Russians, Michel Larionov and Nathalie Gontcharova, gave birth to a short-lived movement called 'Rayonism' which consisted in the decomposition of matter into rays of light. Robert Delaunay and Severini gave their own interpretation of the same concept in France and in Italy. The 'Collage', which is a very important departure in Art, as it constitutes a liberation from paint and accepts any material as medium, flourished at this time. While it would take too long to enumerate all the artists of this movement, one can say that by 1914 Picasso, Braque and Juan Gris were not only at the height of their powers, but had already evolved their particular kind of vision. (I am now speaking only of painters interested in cubism.) It should also be realized that at this time all the arts had come to a point of fusion, and this aided the movement to develop width and gather strength. Guillaume Apollinaire became the poet of the group, Diaghilev, with his theatrical genius, drew around him, and gave inspiration to, many fine artists. Igor Stravinsky contributed musical compositions to the period, notably his ballet, 'L'Oiseau de Feu'. During this very fruitful time all the arts were mutually inspiring. When one looks at a picture painted during this short period, a certain feeling of 'completeness' which transcends visual art can be sensed in it.

Guillaume Apollinaire was killed during the war and the movement lost its poet. The painters who remained alive when the war was over were soon dispersed. Their artistic vision continued to evolve, but they became solitary figures pursuing their separate ways. The movement itself lost its intensity as a group.

However, in retrospect, the unity of purpose and feeling in the movement can be realized, and also the importance it had for the whole visual world of today. For had the revolution of cubism not taken place, the shapes we see every day would probably not have existed. Cars, planes, buildings show the influence of forms discovered by the masters at the beginning of the century, and while it cannot be claimed that they are of cubistic design, they are certainly inspired by it. Moreover, it is a curious fact that a completely naturalistic poster seems somehow out of place today.

Perhaps it is possible to compare the art of the first part of the century to the passing of a circus through the streets of a town. First come the Amazons, the lion tamers, the acrobats, and these are followed by the clowns who imitate their movements and expressions. So it is, maybe, with the arts of today, which are only a reflection of this short, but great, period.

At the present time two of the great exponents of twentieth-century art are still alive; Picasso and Braque. If one searches for harmony, nothing can give it to such an extent as a composition by Braque. The feeling it evokes is a complete vindication of abstract art, if vindication were necessary.

The nature of cubist art is abstract, that is why I speak of cubism and abstract art in the same breath. However, cubism is only one form of it and it has been abandoned now for new forms and experiments. There is one danger that abstract art has escaped, through the very fact of being abstract; soon after its birth it arrived at its inevitable conclusion in the well-known composition of Piet Mondrian. The next step could only be into the void. Abstract artists are therefore safeguarded from absurdity by the logical conclusions of their own theory. Abstract art today is more an enlargement than a continuation.

Fashion and taste

What is fashion and what is taste? And what is the influence of fashion on taste as far as artistic judgment is concerned? We judge a picture with the help of taste. Taste is formed gradually by the development in us of an appreciation of proportion, equilibrium, economy. Our judgment of a picture is also influenced by fashion, for fashion expresses the spirit of the times of which we become a part and which corresponds to what can be described as the general wish of the moment. Taste is therefore a personal achievement. Fashion, on the other hand, is practically outside our control as it depends on a very complicated interrelation between the wishes of the public and the artists. Taste has a measure of permanency. Fashion is entirely transitory. The more we are under the influence of fashion, the less our personal taste is developed.

If we compare the growth of art to a tree, the main branches will represent taste, for they evolve slowly rather than change (remember that our taste in Greek art has not changed). But fashion is like the twigs which sprout, mature, become branches, or just decay. How does this tree live? Taste, like one of the bigger branches, grows and matures independently of the sprigs to which it has given birth, but the sprigs of fashion grow and fight for existence not only against the mother-branch, but against other sprigs, that is, former fashions which are not yet withered. There is, therefore, a three-cornered fight between taste, present fashion and former fashions. The proof of it is the existence of the reactionary school alongside the new school, such as 'fauvism' alongside abstract art. Former fashion feeds itself on the reaction of the public against any new concept and for some time appears as if it might win and destroy the new fashion. Sometimes it indeed happens, but not often, for if the new movement has grown out of a genuine need and gets a measure of approval, and especially if it has artistic value, it will survive.

It has always been said that taste changes. That is not quite exact. Fashion changes and therefore, naturally has a certain influence, however small, on taste. Masterpieces of Giorgione have always remained masterpieces, although they might have been more or less 'in fashion' at certain periods. It is conceivable that while the works of Cézanne might become less fashionable, they could never cease to appeal to people of taste. This change in fashion could come about through the law of supply and demand. We must, however, not minimize the importance of a particular section of the public, for just as well-dressed women influence fashion in clothes, critics and art dealers create fashion in art. It is also true that often, in spite of the critics, art develops in its own free and natural way. For Florentine art flourished alongside Siennese art, which was part of the former fashion, and it was also contemporary with Byzantine art. The impressionists were painting not long after Ingres, and Cézanne and Millet belong to the same period. Every new form of art shows, to a certain extent, the influence of preceding fashions. Of recent years the break with the past has become more pronounced because art has become more intellectual, and therefore more independent, and in consequence every modern school struggles for freedom from former schools. The existence of 'academic' art alongside modern movements has been of great benefit to artists, both as a kind of brake and as a spur.

PART V

Appreciation of Abstract Art

I have given some account of abstract art, and its history. Yet, how to understand it, how to assess its quality and how to obtain pleasure from it are matters that have rarely been considered.

Although the understanding of abstract art follows the same pattern as the understanding of representational art, I feel that it may be helpful, because of the obvious difficulty of mastering abstractions in whatever form they may exist, to try to explain what seems to me to be the mechanism of the understanding of art. It is impossible to lay down any laws on the subject of art appreciation, and I can only speak here of my own conception of it.

We must first agree that understanding is essential to appreciation of art. Understanding, in this connotation, does not mean either intellectual or emotional understanding, the one to the exclusion of the other, but an understanding which unites both and transmutes them into 'intuition'. Jung's philosophical definition of intuition is well known. In artistic matters I should describe it as a perception and comprehension of the object seen at all levels of creation. It is an instantaneous understanding and apprehension—a culmination of a long period of gestation into a single moment.

Rôle of the artist

What is the mechanism of this intuitive understanding of art? We must first deal with the rôle of the artist. At the time of creation the artist gives the totality of his experience and apprehension of the world around him, of which he is a part. He is able to do so because, as an artist, he is the natural yet probably unconscious interpreter of the forces surrounding us, of which we are only very dimly conscious. This act of creation must be total. For, if the artist did not give in his creation the totality of his experience and apprehension, the act would not be artistic creation. Its quality depends on the greatness, skill,

46

mind, spirit, mood and environment of the interpreter: the sum is the artistic personality.

This act of creation which now becomes the work of art is also the gathering into one unit of space (the actual substance of the work of art) and time (the time of creation) of all the diffuse elements that I have mentioned.

To me, this seems to be the only explanation of the change of style by so many artists during the course of their careers. Since if we assume that artistic creation is a fusion of these elements, any change can disturb the balance and alter the nature of the work of art.

Through what medium does the artist come into contact with the spectator? He does it through the representation, of which the outer aspect is the subject. For him, the subject is only a means to an end a pretext for a display of balance of form and colour. But it can be a pretext of a disturbing nature. A subject which is charged with emotion can, through its own inherent meaning, hinder the artist's aim. We know that only the greatest masters, such as Géricault, or Delacroix, could deal with very dramatic subjects without falling into melodrama or banality. This is the reason for the preference of so many painters for still life, which is a first, subconscious, step towards abstraction.

Abstract art also has a subject. It is one, however, that is non-representational. That is, it does not take for pretext an object which is familiar to us, such as a tree, or a human face. The abstract subject is a balance between abstract elements, such as angles, curves and squares, which exist only in our intellects. In other words, the artist has eliminated the first line and the easiest line of contact between his own artistic personality and the spectator, that is, the representational element. Was it necessary? The artist must and can only obey his own laws, it is for us to decide whether we will accept them.

Rôle of the spectator

How do we, spectators, come into contact with the artist? There must be a great difference between the act of creation and the act of understanding or appreciation. The difference lies, to my mind, in the fact that the artist in this one act gives the totality of himself and of his interpretation of the world, while the majority of spectators only accept a facet of this interpretation through a facet of their personality; and this constitutes a meeting point between the artist and themselves. I speak now of the majority of spectators, as it is obvious that the aim of every art lover should be to multiply his points of contact, widen his field of appreciation, in other words 'depersonalize' his taste.

We are not in complete unison with the artist, because although he gives us his complete self, it is gathered in one unit of creation, time and space. We receive his interpretation only with facets of our personalities, yet we are at liberty to choose from an infinite variety of sources, that is from any artist and works of art. It is this gap between creation and appreciation that we must try to bridge. This can only be done by constant looking at art, whether abstract or representational.

With the suppression of a representational subject, and the substitution of an abstract subject, contact must become more difficult. We find ourselves in contact with the artistic personality of the artist, on the level of unfamiliar abstractions, without an introduction. We are faced with his inner world, without the help— to which we have been conditioned all our lives—of a concrete object. Yet our aim is exactly this: to come face to face with the artist's inner world. The suppression of the representational element is an added difficulty to the understanding; yet it can also be a help. Now that the initial stage of the first contact has been disposed of, the spectator finds himself confronted with balance of form and colour, and relationships between elements may become clearer. Composition, which can be lost through the potency of the subject, may emerge. The spectator is undisturbed; and is taken into the cool world of ideas in which harmony reigns supreme.

How do we approach this understanding? There is one way only: through participation with the artist. It is true that the appreciation of abstract art demands a great intellectual effort, that is, meeting the artist half-way, going intellectually and consciously towards him. The meeting takes place at a different level. We must never dogmatize about art. Apart from the non-representational element of abstract art, all art is fundamentally one. In every representational painting we look for a feeling of the abstract; in most abstract works we search for a link with the experienced world. Most great painters have at times been representational and abstract in the same composition. This was certainly often so with Klee. Some, like Mondrian and Malevitch, have evolved into abstraction. Others, like Picasso, have many times returned to representational painting.

Assessment of abstract art
How can we, therefore, assess the quality of an abstract painting? Every work of art, be it representational or abstract, must finally be judged through the

harmonious balance of each of its elements with each other; and that the total effect of these elements should also be harmonious. Naturally, many other qualities are necessary to make a work of art; but it would be impossible to discuss them here.

When we come to the assessment of a work we tend, however distasteful it may be, to make comparisons. In representational art, if we try for instance, to compare two pictures representing the flight of angels, we can isolate the abstract element, which is flight, or movement, and debate which of the two compositions renders it best. With abstract art this is not so easy. Each element being an absolute, elements can only be judged within themselves. On the other hand, while a representational painting can be appreciated in isolation, to my mind, an abstract work needs the environment and support of its own world—the abstract world. For it is part of a wide yet specific visualization.

Enjoyment of abstract art

How can we take pleasure in abstract art? If we assume that understanding and assessment are necessary components of pleasure, we can rightly say that, having understood and assessed it, a certain pleasure must be inevitable. Yet pleasure is personal and indefinable. Pleasure in abstract art is difficult to attain, since it lacks passion and emotion. Yet no enjoyment can be derived from a work of art if passion and emotion are obliterated altogether. In the case of abstract art, these emotions are lifted into another sphere, and transmuted on to a different, more intellectual, level. It is precisely the emotionless quality of abstract art which invests it with a peculiar power to move us. It could be said that abstract art is to representational art what philosophy is to the novel. Yet there are many novels of which the philosophical meaning is of greater depth than that of many strictly philosophical concepts. This applies also to art. We should not allow ourselves to be dogmatically swayed towards abstraction, nor stubbornly refuse to allow ourselves to leave the representational level. Both are merely mediums which in the end reflect the greatness of the artist.

Future of abstract art

What of the future of abstract art? If we agree that art is the verdict of the world around us, we can, by using our eyes and our intuition, have an idea of the direction that art is likely to take. Also, we must not forget that in every great artist we see not only the present but a prophecy of future forms. It is for us to try to develop this prophetic quality, and we can only do so through constant contact with art.

If I have put much emphasis on abstract art, in comparison with other schools, it is because I feel that this development is more significant in the history of art than any other form of artistic achievement. If I have used philosophical terms to try to explain it, it is because I feel that it is only through the intellect that one can attempt to understand it; and that, therefore, the philosophical approach is the most fitting.

High Water-Wood by Paul Klee. *Private Collection*
(See pages 20 and 51)

PART VI

Other Forms of Modern Painting

There are, as everyone knows, other forms of modern art; there are surrealism, symbolism and fauvism and also constructivism and futurism, which are derivatives of abstract art, as they change objects into abstract images.

Surrealism
Surrealism taken in a literal sense is the expression of the artist's inner sensations without taking into account any artistic values. It could be described as automatic painting. This is naturally only a partial definition, as anyone who attempts to express his inner sensations through art must be, in effect, artistic. It is obvious, therefore, that the quality of a surrealist picture will depend not only on the quality of the artist's inner sensations, but on the degree of his artistic sense. However, since the concept of surrealism is related both to naturalism and abstraction, it is often in danger of losing balance, and lapsing into exaggeration of one kind or another.

Symbolism
Symbolism, which is very akin to surrealism, bears, however, relation to reality. Chagall tried to express through symbols the sufferings of the Jews in Russia, and in doing so has shown a particular kind of Christian feeling which is unknown to the West. His pictures have not only great charm but they also touch a chord of emotion in us which forms a link between the spectator and the artist.

The symbolism of Klee, who died in 1940, is perhaps the most personal form of art of the present day. It is very different from that of Chagall, as it is neither human nor religious, for the feelings he discovers in human beings and transposes pictorially to the canvas in minute lines, belong to a psychological region unexplored as yet by any artist. Although Klee has created no school—probably because he has said the last word in his peculiar form of art—he has perhaps had more influence than any other painter on the artistic vision of today. It is especially at the present time, when a new orientation in taste is taking place that it is most felt—but it is not within the scope of this book to discuss present tendencies.

It is difficult to place Rouault in any group. He is like one of those lone spirits whom no one dares to follow for fear of being exposed to too much intensity of feeling. He could be called an obsessed painter, for he seems obsessed with the personalities of circus dancers and clowns, and the expression of suffering on their faces. He is also a Christian painter, but being a Catholic, his approach to religion is different from Chagall's, whose religious feeling is under the influence of the East European attitude to God.

The discovery of psychoanalysis and the interest this aroused in the sub-conscious are probably mainly responsible for the growth of both surrealism and symbolism. Surrealism is not in itself a new mode of art. Hieronymus Bosch, a Flemish painter of the fifteenth century was indeed a true surrealist, with his vivid depiction of strange creatures and monsters, the inhabitants of a realm of the imagination very far removed from the conventional reality of daily life. The same is true of the Italian painter, Traini, who is perhaps the painter of the fresco, 'The Triumph of Death' (now in the Museum at Pisa), in which Death's victory over Life is symbolized by a cavalcade of gentlefolk who are shown the futility of pomp and riches by being faced with corpses and skeletons in gaping graves. The difference between the earlier forms of surrealism and symbolism in painting and those of today is that, while the earlier examples are more obvious, probably because they were designed for the propagation of the Faith, and therefore con-formed to definite conventions, the artists of today suffer no such restrictions. They have not only been released from the church, but have also been encouraged to delve into the depths of their subconscious. Psychologically, the artist is now nearer self-expression.

But in whatever mode it is painted, every work of art must be judged on the harmony between its various elements and their balance.

The 'Fauves'

The 'Fauves' are perhaps the direct heirs of the impressionists. This is because, although they re-acted against them, they did so only in technique but not in feeling. They believed that colour is the only element that gives pictorial worth to a picture. Their danger is excess of colour, which is what happened to 'expressionism', especially in Germany and Scandinavia. In the case of the

German expressionists, this chromatic exaggeration may be due to their natural temperament, which is sometimes prone to excess. The greatest exponent of the 'fauve' school was Matisse, and it is only his innate taste and disciplined restraint in choosing his gradations of colour that have saved him from the excesses into which so many other painters of this school have often fallen. In a picture by Matisse, one can see how the colours are skilfully and tastefully led away from the centre to the borders of the painting, for every shade is applied so that it will not lose its value through the vicinity of any other colour. Matisse said of himself that he had no preconceived idea. He paints in the yellow of a chair, and 'builds' around it. His self-criticism is useful, but in studying his work the influence he derived from the abstract movement must also be remembered, that is, orderliness and the use of 'absolutes'. Matisse was neither a religious painter nor a painter with a 'message'. The church he decorated in the South of France has little religious feeling in it and the nuns have great trouble in keeping the tourists from talking out loud, which does not happen in the church decorated by Rouault in Savoie. Matisse has said of painting that it was designed as a relaxation for business men and should be enjoyed from the armchair. This remark describes the character of his art.

Microscopic art

A form of artistic representation which has a deceptive appearance of abstract art in this category is microscopic art. Through the microscope, a new world of living beings and minute detail of the structure of matter have become familiar to us, and artists, always in search of new forms, have represented them, and often based their designs upon them. The microscope has, like the aeroplane, given us a new vision of the world which has now become part of artistic vision, as any fresh view must sooner or later become part of the vision of the artists of the time.

Both the microscope and the aeroplane have helped us to see in a 'patterned way', for whether one is looking at the infinitely small through lenses, or at a wide expanse from the sky, what one sees is a recurring pattern. Certain abstract compositions by Paul Klee are reminiscent of forests and vegetation seen from the air, and they also remind one of objects seen under the microscope.

PART VII

How to Look at Paintings

Distance

The distance from which a picture is looked at is of great importance. Certain paintings can be rightly seen near to, others only from afar. In fact, there is a right distance from which to look at every picture. Although this right distance depends to some extent on the spectator, it is understandable that while 'old masters can be looked at from a distance difficult to define impressionists pictures can only be properly seen from a certain definite distance. The distance is correct when the colours which the impressionists have used become 'a whole' in the eye of the onlooker, thus allowing the forms to emerge. The same applies to divisionist painting which demands its own distance, in order to be adequately seen.

Every painting, in principle, has its own 'distance'. It is for the spectator to find it.

The Contact

When one looks at a painting there is an initial contact. This can be thought of as similar to the first contact one has with a human being, because a work of art has within it a mysterious life of its own. One of the main objects of an artist is to transmit something of the life he has in him on to his canvas. If this has been satisfactorily achieved the painting is 'a thing alive'. The first contact is in its nature a sudden experience. It shows at once whether there is anything in common between the spectator and the artist. The more the spectator is artistically awakened, or educated, the more correct will be his first impression.

The second stage of looking at a picture is to take in every detail. Details, which at first glance seem irrelevant, are nevertheless part of the artist's whole conception. It is often necessary to seek out the details with the eye, for unless deliberately looked for, many may be missed. The obvious way is to begin by looking at the centre of interest, and letting the eye be led naturally first towards the depth, then the sides of the painting, the vision being guided by the successful arrangement of values, volumes and masses. One must get into the habit of looking at paintings three-dimensionally. I am now speaking of representational pictures. The eye should also be led from the important towards the less important. When one looks at a portrait by Holbein, the first thing one naturally sees is the mouth, then the eyes, because it is on the mouth primarily and on the eyes secondly that Holbein concentrated all his powers of portraiture. Only when a painting has been seen as a whole, and all its qualities grasped, can the discussion of its faults and merits begin.

Development of taste

In order to understand the qualities that make a work of art 'great' and to be discerning about them, we must develop one all-important quality, namely, our taste, and the best way to develop taste is to *look at* pictures. But to look at pictures, one must know how to see them. Everyone should take advantage of whatever is within his reach. Those who live in Great Britain, and especially in London, have perhaps the best and rarest art treasures at their disposal. The National Gallery, the Tate Gallery, the Victoria and Albert Museum, the British Museum, without speaking of smaller collections, such as that at the Dulwich Gallery, have perhaps between them the finest and best selected examples of painting in the world. This is owing to the non-nationalistic and non-sectarian attitude of those in charge of the national collections and of private collectors. The same cannot be said of all other countries.

One cannot be urged to do anything more useful and more rewarding than learn how to look and how to see.